THE WORLD
IN THE TIME OF
MARIE ANTOINETTE

Dillon Press
Parsippany, New Jersey

FIONA MACDONALD

First published in the UK in 1997 by
Belitha Press Limited, London House, Great Eastern Wharf,
Parkgate Road, London SW11 4NQ

Copyright in this format © Belitha Press Limited 1997
Text by Fiona Macdonald
Map by Robin Carter, Wildlife Art Agency

Published in the United States in 1998 by

Dillon Press
A Division of Simon & Schuster
299 Jefferson Road
Parsippany, New Jersey 07054-0480

Library of Congress Cataloging-in-Publication Data
Macdonald, Fiona.
   The world in the time of Marie Antoinette / Fiona Macdonald.
      p.   cm. — (The world in the time of series)
   Simultaneously published: London, Eng. : Belitha Press, 1997.
   Includes index.
   Summary: Recounts the story of Marie Antoinette and looks at what was
happening all around the world in her time.
   1. Marie Antoinette, Queen, consort of Louis XVI, King of France,
1755-1793—Juvenile literature.   2. Queens—France—Biography—Juvenile
literature.   3. Civilization, Modern—18th century—Juvenile literature.
4. France—Civilization—18th century—Juvenile literature.   5. France—
History—Revolution, 1789-1799—Juvenile literature.   6. Regicides—France—
Juvenile literature.   7. Social change—Juvenile literature.   [1. Marie Antoinette,
Queen, consort of Louis XVI, King of France, 1755-1793.   2. Kings, queens,
rulers, etc.   3. France—History—Revolution, 1789-1799.   4. Civilization,
Modern—18th century.] I. Title. II. Series.
DC137.1.M33   1998
909'.7—dc21   97-22085

ISBN 0-382-39735-5 (LSB)   10 9 8 7 6 5 4 3 2 1
ISBN 0-382-39734-7 (PBK)   10 9 8 7 6 5 4 3 2 1

Editor: Christine Hatt
Design: Jamie Asher
Picture Researcher: Diana Morris
Consultant: Sallie Purkis

Printed in Hong Kong

Picture acknowledgments:

AKG London: front cover r SMPK Kunstbibliothek Berlin; title page & 4; 5t
Akademie der Bilden Kuenste Vienna; 5b Palais de Versailles; 6b; 7t Bibliothèque
Nationale Paris; 13t Heeresgeschichtliches Museum Vienna; 13b; 18
Niederschsisches Landesmuseum Hannover; 19t Russian Museum St. Petersburg;
24; title page 28b Biblioteca del Palacio Real Madrid; 31t, 31b, 34.

Bridgeman Art Library: front cover c & 6t V & A Museum London; 7b
Giraudon/Musée de la Ville de Paris, Musée Carnavalet; 15b British Library; 16
Roy Miles Gallery, 29 Bruton Street, London W1; 17t National Library of
Australia Canberra; 22 Brooklyn Museum NY; 23b National Library of Australia
Canberra; 25b Christies London; 27t V & A Museum London; 27b British
Museum London; 28t Musée de la Co-operation Franco-Americaine; 29 Mitchell
Library NSW; 30 NMM London; 36 Schloss Schonbrunn Vienna; 37t The
Hermitage St. Petersburg; 37b Christies London; 40 Derby Museum & Art
Gallery; 41l Private Collection; 42 Museo Correr Venice; title page & 43b V & A
Museum London; 45 National Library of Australia Canberra. **Jean-Loup
Charmet:** 25t. **Corbis-Bettmann:** 39. **ET Archive:** 21b Musée Guimet Paris;
32t V & A Museum London; 33t; front cover cl & 38r Marco Polo Gallery Paris;
41r Private Collection. **Werner Forman Archive**: front cover l & 14 British
Museum London; 15t; contents & 20 Wallace Collection London; 35t Canterbury
Museum Christchurch; 38l British Museum London. **Robert Harding Picture
Library:** 21t, 44t. **Images of India:** 43t Ilay Cooper. **National Maritime
Museum London:** 12. **Natural History Museum London:** 35b. **Peter
Newark's Pictures:** 17b, 23t, 44b. **North Wind Picture Archive:** 19b, 26.
Wellcome Centre Medical Photographic Library: 33b.

CONTENTS

ABOUT THIS BOOK

This book tells the story of Marie Antoinette and looks at what was happening all around the world in her time. To help you find your way through the book, each chapter has been divided into seven sections. Each section describes a different part of the world and is headed by a color bar. As you look through a chapter, the color bars tell you which areas you can read about in the text below. There is a time line, to give you an outline of world events in Marie Antoinette's time, and also a map, which shows some of the most important places mentioned in this book.

On page 46 there is a list of some of the peoples you will read about in this book. Some of the more unfamiliar words are also listed in the glossary.

THE STORY OF MARIE ANTOINETTE

► This glamorous portrait of Marie Antoinette was painted in 1778, when she had been Queen of France for four years. Marie Antoinette employed the top French designers, like Rose Bertin, to make her elaborate clothes. They set the fashion and were copied by noblewomen in many lands.

Queen Marie Antoinette lived in France just over 200 years ago. At the start of her life, she was surrounded by love and luxury—but she died a prisoner, hated by millions of ordinary people and deserted by most of her rich friends. This book will tell you about life in Marie Antoinette's France, and what was happening elsewhere in the world during Marie Antoinette's time. As Marie Antoinette's life was short—she died in 1793, aged only 37—this book looks at a longer time span, from about 1700 to 1800. This will help you to find out more about the people, ideas, and events that shaped the world Marie Antoinette knew and to discover what happened in the years just after she died.

POWERFUL FAMILY

Archduchess Marie Antoinette Josèphe Jeanne was born on November 2, 1755, into Europe's most powerful royal family. Her mother, Maria Theresa, was Empress of the Austrian Empire and ruled most of Central Europe. Her father, Francis I, was Duke of Lorraine and also had the title Holy Roman Emperor. This gave him authority over many European kingdoms.

Marie Antoinette grew up in the royal palace in Vienna, the capital of Austria. She was not clever, but she was lively, pretty, and fond of music, dancing, theater, and the other arts. From a young age she was trained to be the wife of a great man. She learned how to present a good public image and to be charming to visitors.

▲ Empress Maria Theresa of Austria with some of her many children on the terrace of the royal palace at Schönbrunn, near Vienna in Austria

ARRANGED MARRIAGE

Empress Maria Theresa and Emperor Francis arranged marriages for their children. When Marie Antoinette was growing up, Maria Theresa wanted to make an alliance with France. So, in 1770, Marie Antoinette married Prince Louis, the young heir to the French throne. Louis was not interested in politics or economics, even though a successful ruler needed to understand both of these subjects. But in 1774, when he was 20, he was crowned King Louis XVI of France. Marie Antoinette, aged only 19, became queen.

▶ Prince Louis of France was tall, plump, shy, good-natured, and dull. His main interests were hunting, food, and metalwork.

FAMILY LIFE

Marie Antoinette found her husband and life at court boring. She spent most of her time with her friends and neglected her duties. The French began to say that she was a silly foreigner who spent too much. Her popularity increased after her first child was born in 1778. When two more babies followed, Louis was glad. He preferred family life to state affairs.

GOSSIP AND SCANDAL

It was not long before unfriendly gossip about Marie Antoinette started again. From 1785 to 1786 a scandal known as the Affair of the Diamond Necklace rocked France. Many people believed that Marie Antoinette had persuaded a priest to steal a diamond necklace for her, in return for promises of love. In fact, she was totally innocent, but the reputation of the royal family was still badly damaged.

◀ Marie Antoinette spent her childhood surrounded by beautiful things. When she moved to France, she was delighted to find that French craft workers were among the best in Europe, producing fine furniture, porcelain, silks, and lace. This porcelain jug and bowl were made in the French factory of Sèvres in 1763. They are decorated in pure gold.

SERIOUS PROBLEMS

Even before Louis XVI became king in 1774, France faced serious problems. They grew worse during his reign. There were demands for changes in the way France was governed, a terrible financial crisis, and poverty and hunger in the countryside. Shut away in the palace, amusing herself with her elegant friends, Marie Antoinette did nothing to help. There was probably little she could have done, because her husband and his advisors did not want change. But her frivolous, expensive lifestyle angered many politicians and ordinary people throughout France.

REVOLUTION!

In 1789 the French people's anger exploded into a revolution. (You can read more about this on page 13.) In July, crowds attacked the Bastille, an ancient prison in the center of Paris. Then, in October, they marched on the royal palace at Versailles, some distance from the capital. King Louis, Marie Antoinette, and their three children were forced to move to an older, smaller palace in Paris itself. There they were kept under armed guard. To try to restore peace, King Louis agreed to all the protesters' demands. But he did not really intend to reform the government. At the same time he allowed Marie Antoinette to write secretly to her family in Austria. She asked them for help to put an end to the French Revolution and to restore the royal family's power.

◀ In October 1789 a mob of poor women market traders marched from Paris to attack the royal family in their palace at Versailles. After a year of economic crisis and serious shortages of food, they demanded bread to feed their families and lower taxes.

▲ King Louis and Queen Marie Antoinette were recognized as they tried to escape, and soldiers loyal to the revolution took them prisoner.

ESCAPE ATTEMPT

In 1791, King Louis, Marie Antoinette, and their children disguised themselves in servants' clothes and escaped from the palace at night. They hurried toward Belgium, where Marie Antoinette's brother was waiting with an army, ready to rescue them. But their bid to win freedom failed. Just a few miles away from the border, King Louis was recognized by a local postmaster, who had seen his portrait on banknotes. The king and his family were arrested and taken back to a Paris prison in disgrace.

▶ The guillotine was designed as a humane alternative to hanging. But during the French Revolution, it proved to be a deadly machine for mass executions. It was used to kill not only the king and queen, but also thousands of nobles, priests, and supporters of the royal family.

VICTIMS OF THE GUILLOTINE

Early in 1792 the Austrians invaded France. They wanted to put an end to the revolution and free Louis and Marie Antoinette. But they were forced to retreat. In August the leaders of the revolution declared that the king and queen no longer had the right to rule, and that France was to become a republic. In December, Louis was tried for "crimes against the state." He was found guilty and publicly guillotined on January 21, 1793.

Marie Antoinette remained in prison for a few months more. But soon she, too, was put on trial. Revolutionary leaders accused her of treason. They said that she had plotted secretly against the revolution and had encouraged the Austrians, who were enemies of France. They found her guilty and sentenced her to death. She was eventually executed by guillotine on October 16, 1793.

THE WORLD 1700–1800

ABOUT THE MAPS

The maps on this page will help you find your way around the world in Marie Antoinette's time. The big map shows some of the places mentioned in the text, including:

• **COUNTRIES** that are different from modern ones, such as Persia, as well as some important states and regions.

• *Peoples*, such as the Seneca. The descendants of these peoples often live in the same place today, but their traditional lifestyles have almost vanished.

• *GEOGRAPHICAL FEATURES*, including mountains and rivers.

• *Towns and cities.* To find the position of a town or city, look for the name in the list below and then find the number on the map.

1 Williamsburg	8 Istanbul	15 Yangôn
2 Montreal	9 Djenné	16 Bangkok
3 Quebec	10 Timbuktu	17 Penang
4 Bath	11 Amritsar	18 Qufu
5 Paris	12 Jaipur	19 Guangzhou
6 Vienna	13 Delhi	20 Nagasaki
7 St. Petersburg	14 Calcutta	

The little map shows the world divided into seven regions. The people who lived in a region were linked by customs, traditions, beliefs, or simply by their environment. There were many differences within each region, but the people living there had more in common with one another than with people elsewhere. Each region is shown in a different color. The same colors are used in the headings throughout the book.

ARCTIC
OCEAN

SIBERIA

BERING STRAIT

BALTIC
SEA   7
PRUSSIA

EUROPE

4

5   AUSTRIAN
EMPIRE   6

OTTOMAN   8   BLACK
EMPIRE   SEA

CASPIAN
SEA
CAUCASUS
MOUNTAINS

ASIA

Kirghiz

MEDITERRANEAN
SEA

PERSIA

HIMALAYA
MOUNTAINS

18

MT. FUJI

20

AFRICA

10
9

NILE R.

PUNJAB   11 13
          12
          MOGUL
          EMPIRE   14
          Marathas

BENGAL
ANNAM   19
BURMA
15   Mons
SIAM
16

PACIFIC

OCEAN

Fulani
Hausa

Bambara
Yoruba
Ashanti Bini

Dinka

17

Buganda

EQUATOR

Masai

Luanda

Aborigines

AUSTRALASIA

KALAHARI
DESERT
Khoikhoi
Xhosa
CAPE
COLONY

NEW
HOLLAND

CAPE OF
GOOD HOPE

Maoris

KEY TO MAP

Africa

Americas

Australasia

East Asia

Europe

Middle East

South Asia

EQUATOR

TIME LINE

1700   1725

EUROPE

1700–1721 Russia and Sweden fight Great Northern War for control of far northern Europe.

1701–1714 War of the Spanish Succession

1702 First English-language daily newspaper, *The Daily Courant*, published in London.

1703 Peter the Great of Russia founds St. Petersburg.

1707 England and Scotland unite to form Great Britain.

1714 German Gabriel Fahrenheit invents mercury-filled thermometer.

1715 First Jacobite rebellion in Scotland. Supporters of Stuart dynasty oppose new British ruling family, the Hanoverians.

1727 British mathematician and astronomer Sir Isaac Newton dies, aged 85.

1735 Swedish scientist Carolus Linnaeus invents a new system of classifying plants and animals.

1740–1786 Frederick the Great rules Prussia.

1745 Second Jacobite rebellion in Scotland.

MIDDLE EAST

1710–1774 Series of wars between Ottoman Turkey and Russia.

1729–1732 War between Persians and Afghans.

c.1735 Wahhabi religious reform movement begins in Arabia.

1736–1747 Reign of Nadir Shah in Persia.

1737–1747 Persians invade Afghanistan.

AFRICA

1700 Ashanti kingdom becomes powerful in West Africa.

1705 Tunis wins independence from Ottoman rule.

c.1710 Algeria becomes independent from Ottoman rule.

1711 Tripoli wins independence from Ottoman rule.

c.1730 Kingdom of Borno becomes powerful in Sudan.

1747–1748 Yoruba people of Nigeria conquer nearby Dahomey and Benin.

SOUTH ASIA

c.1711 Dutch settlers in East Indies begin to set up coffee plantations.

1707 Mogul Empire begins to collapse after death of Emperor Aurangzeb.

1714 Maratha princes begin to become powerful in central India.

1739 Persian ruler Nadir Shah attacks city of Delhi.

EAST ASIA

1715 China invades Mongolia.

1720 China conquers Tibet.

1736–1796 Reign of Chinese emperor Qianlong.

1703 Over 200,000 people die in Japanese earthquake.

AMERICAS

1701 Peace treaty between French settlers and Native Americans in northeastern North America.

1702–1713 War between European settlers and Native Americans.

1728–1733 Dane Vitus Bering explores Alaska.

1738 George Whitefield begins Great Awakening religious movement in North America.

1744–1748 King George's War between French and English settlers in North America.

AUSTRALASIA

1699–1701 British explorer William Dampier travels along coastline of Australia and Papua New Guinea.

1721–1722 Dutch explorer Jacob Roggeveen travels to Samoa, the Solomon Islands, and Easter Island.

1750   **1775**   **1800**

1751–1780 French scholar Denis Diderot publishes his Encyclopedia.

1756–1763 Seven Years' War

1762–1796 Catherine the Great rules Russia.

1755 Marie Antoinette born.

1770 British inventor James Hargreaves patents spinning jenny to spin woolen thread.

1773 Cossack rebellion led by Pugachev in Russia.

1765 Scottish scientist James Watt invents steam engine.

1789 French Revolution begins.

1790 Italian doctor Luigi Galvani investigates electricity.

1793 Queen Marie Antoinette and King Louis XVI executed.

1799 Army general Napoleon seizes power in France.

1787–1792 Russia conquers all Ottoman lands to north of Black Sea.

1763 Wahhabi religious leaders begin to take control of Arabia.

1793 Sultan Selim III reforms Ottoman Empire.

1799 Napoleon invades Holy Land.

1770 Scottish explorer James Bruce reaches source of Blue Nile River.

c.1776–1786 Fulani people set up Muslim states in West Africa.

1790 Buganda kingdom expands in East Africa.

1795 British troops occupy Cape of Good Hope.

1779–1781 and 1793 Wars between Xhosa people of southern Africa and Boer (Dutch) settlers.

1798 Napoleon invades Egypt.

1755–1756 King Alaungpaya begins to unite Burma and founds Rangoon.

1757 Britain defeats troops from Bengal at Battle of Plassey.

1782 Rama I becomes king of Siam.

1758 Marathas capture Punjab.

1786 Britain gains control of Penang, Malaysia.

1767–1769 China invades Burma and demands tribute.

1791–1792 War between China and Tibet.

1775 Chinese population reaches about 264 million.

1793 Chinese refuse British request to trade.

1751 Benjamin Franklin's experiments with electricity.

1759 Britain captures Quebec in Canada.

1776 American Declaration of Independence

1789 George Washington becomes first President of U.S.

1780–1781 Revolt led by Tupac Amaru II against Spanish in Peru.

1791 Revolt by slaves in Haiti led by Toussaint L'Ouverture.

1763 Britain wins control of Canada, lands east of the Mississippi River from France, and Florida from Spain.

1783 Peace treaty ends American Revolution.

1793 Eli Whitney invents cotton gin.

1769 Captain Cook reaches New Zealand.

1788 Britain transports first convicts to Australia.

1770 Captain Cook claims New Holland (New South Wales in Australia) for Britain.

1779 Captain Cook killed in Hawaii.

1793 First free settlers arrive in Australia.

Many of the dates shown in this Time Line are approximate. The letter c. stands for the Latin word *circa*, and means "about."

AROUND THE WORLD

The world changed dramatically between 1700 and 1800. Kings and queens, like Louis XVI and Marie Antoinette, were toppled from their thrones, and conquered peoples and colonies began to demand the right to govern themselves. Bigger ships, better navigation techniques, and a new spirit of curiosity led to more contacts between countries. Most links were made through trade. This was sometimes of a shameful sort, particularly when millions of Africans were transported across the Atlantic Ocean as slaves. Meanwhile European soldiers, missionaries, and explorers began to spread European power around the globe.

▲ East Indiamen were cargo ships that sailed between Europe and the Far East. Cotton, sugar, and other exotic goods from Asia and the Americas were rarely found in Europe in 1700. But by 1800, thanks to ships like these, they could be bought there quite cheaply and easily.

CONSTANT WARFARE

Throughout the 1700s many nations in Europe were almost constantly at war. Austria, France, and Prussia were the strongest and richest. When one of them grew too strong and threatened to take control of Europe, the other two fought against it together. This was called "keeping the balance of power." Smaller nations often got involved in the fighting, too. In northern Europe there was a similar struggle between Sweden and Russia for control of the countries around the Baltic Sea.

▲ This flag was carried by Prussian soldiers during the Seven Years' War (1756–1763) against Austria and France. The Latin motto in the center means "For glory and homeland."

THE FRENCH REVOLUTION

France faced many problems when Marie Antoinette was queen (see pages 4–7). By 1789, King Louis XVI's failure to find solutions led to a revolution. The leaders of the revolution wanted to end poverty and hunger and to introduce fair government. From September 1793 to July 1794, extremists like lawyer Maximilien Robespierre organized a Reign of Terror, in which about 15,000 "enemies of the revolution" were guillotined. After the king and queen were executed in 1793, revolutionary leaders tried to spread their ideas of liberty and equality by conquering other European lands. So their rulers declared war on France and refused to buy French goods. The commander of the French army was Napoleon Bonaparte, and in 1799 he took over the government of France, too.

OTTOMAN DEFEAT

MIDDLE EAST

Terrible wars were also fought in many Middle Eastern countries. Between 1710 and 1774, Russia and the powerful Ottoman sultans of Turkey fought three times for control of territory around the Black and Caspian Seas. In 1774, Russia defeated the Ottomans. Most Russian harbors were blocked by ice in winter, but this victory gave them access to warm-water ports on the Black Sea that did not freeze over. The Russian Orthodox Church—closely linked to the Russian government—also gained the right to represent Christians living in Ottoman lands.

AFGHANS AND PERSIANS

In 1722, Afghan troops occupied the neighboring country of Persia (present-day Iran). In 1732, the Persians managed to drive them out. Then, led by new ruler Nadir Shah (see page 19), they captured Iraq and parts of Russia. In 1739 the Persians successfully invaded India, conquering much of the North and West.

▼ Russian soldiers defeating the Turkish army at the Battle of Kagul in 1770

GREAT EMPIRES

AFRICA

West Africa was home to many great empires during the 1700s—the Ashanti of present-day Ghana, the Bambara of Nigeria, and the Yoruba of Dahomey and Benin. They all grew rich through trading in gold, metalwork, ivory, and slaves. Farther to the south, the Luanda people founded a kingdom in the rain forests of Central Africa. In southeastern Africa, the hunting and cattle-herding Masai people expanded their control over a vast area of savannah land. In and around the region of present-day Uganda, the Buganda kingdom also seized control of new territories.

▲ Magnificent gold jewelry, decorated with leaves and flowers, was worn by senior government officials at the Ashanti kings' court. Many African kingdoms grew rich through trading in gold.

THE SLAVE TRADE

A form of slavery had existed in many parts of Africa for thousands of years. Most slaves in these traditional societies were either criminals or prisoners of war. But by 1750 the old laws regulating slavery had been swept away. European merchants demanded at least 45,000 slaves a year from traders in West Africa. Families, even whole villages, were rounded up and marched to the coast. Lives were wrecked and communities destroyed. Historians estimate that between 6 and 7 million African men, women, and children were transported across the Atlantic Ocean between 1700 and 1800 to work as slaves in the Americas.

COLONY ON THE CAPE

In 1652, Jan van Riebeeck and some other Dutch farmers had founded the first European colony on the Cape of Good Hope, at the tip of southern Africa. By 1700 their descendants were beginning to explore farther inland. They settled in sheltered, fertile river valleys, planted vineyards, and had cattle farms. In 1795, British troops captured the Cape Colony from the Dutch.

MOGULS IN DECLINE

SOUTH ASIA

Since about 1526, the magnificent Mogul dynasty of Muslim emperors had ruled India. But by the 1700s, Mughal power was fading. European merchant companies—especially those of the British and French—controlled the most profitable parts of Indian trade, together with large areas of Indian land. Local Indian princes, such as the Marathas of central India and the Sikhs of the Punjab region in the north, took advantage of the Moguls' weakness to set up kingdoms of their own. India was also invaded twice in the eighteenth century, by the Persians in 1739 and the Afghans in 1761.

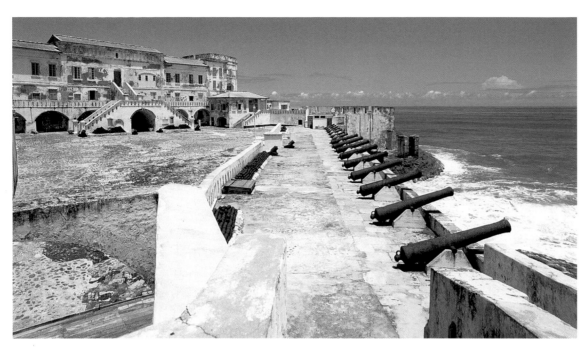

◄ Forts like this were built to house the many European merchants who traded along the west coast of Africa and to store valuable "goods," including slaves.

EUROPEANS IN INDIA

The British and the French were rivals in India. Troops of the British East India Company, led by an ambitious young businessman, Robert Clive, defeated the French army in a series of battles between 1751 and 1763.

British soldiers also fought against local Indian princes. In 1756, the Nawab (ruler) of Bengal, the richest region of India, imprisoned 146 British people in a tiny dungeon. Many died of suffocation. British people in India were outraged, and the prison became known as the Black Hole of Calcutta. In 1757, Clive and his troops defeated the Nawab at the Battle of Plassey, and Bengal came under British control.

Between 1775 and 1782, the British and the Maratha princes were also at war. But the East India Company used peaceful negotiations to win the right to collect taxes on behalf of the Mogul emperors in many other Indian states.

EXPANSION OF TRADE

The British East India Company was not active in India alone. In 1700 it established a trading post in Borneo (in present-day Indonesia) and in 1786 built a larger trading settlement in Penang, Malaysia. Company members were eager to make profits from Asian spices, jewels, and drugs.

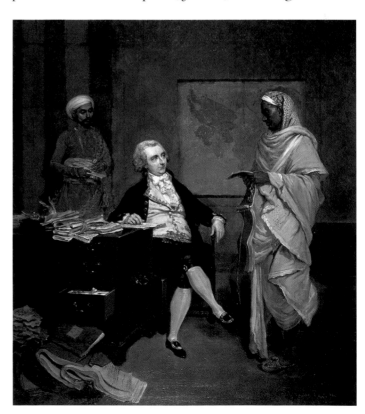

► This scene from 1790 shows John Mowbray, a British East India Company merchant, in his office with his financial advisor.

FAMOUS RULERS AND LEADERS

In the time of Marie Antoinette, people in many parts of the world began to ask questions about how they should be governed. Who had the right to rule? Were kings and queens appointed by God? Should they inherit their role? Or should they be chosen by ordinary people? Did every country have the right to govern itself? Or did powerful nations have the right to colonize or occupy other countries? And what about laws? Should they be based on religious beliefs, ancient traditions, or decisions made in parliaments elected by the people? All these questions were fiercely discussed in the 1700s. But different rulers and leaders had different ideas about how they should be answered.

◀ King Frederick the Great of Prussia (ruled 1740–1786) was a brilliant army commander. He made Prussia the second most powerful state in Europe, after its rival, Austria.

◄ Empress Catherine the Great of Russia (ruled 1762–1796) was a remarkable woman. At home she punished her critics harshly. Abroad she led successful army campaigns, conquering new territory and making Russia rich and strong.

NADIR SHAH

MIDDLE EAST

Nadir Shah of Persia was born in 1688, the son of a chieftain in the wild frontier lands between Persia and Afghanistan. He won fame as a brilliant cavalry officer, fighting alongside the Persians to drive out Afghan armies from their land. By 1732, when the Afghans were defeated, Nadir Shah controlled all Persia. The king, Abbas III, was still a baby, so Nadir Shah made himself regent and ruled in his place. He attacked Iraq, controlled by the Ottomans, in 1733, and then conquered Russian land in the Caucasus Mountains. In 1736 he deposed Abbas and declared himself king. In 1739 he invaded India, occupied the capital city of Delhi, and seized vast amounts of treasure from its Mogul palaces.

ROYAL RULERS

EUROPE

Marie Antoinette's parents in Austria and her husband's family in France, Frederick the Great of Prussia, and Catherine the Great of Russia, were all typical European rulers of the 1700s. They believed that they had the absolute right to govern their countries and that people should obey them without question.

These monarchs took all power into their own hands and ignored the advice of assemblies of nobles and wealthy citizens. Instead they appointed their own advisors and government officials and often controlled the army, too. They also kept magnificent courts and held ceremonies that displayed their power. Some of these rulers did introduce social and educational reforms. But their refusal to let people share in government led to trouble and, in France, to revolution.

► Nadir Shah, ruler of Persia, was successful, but totally ruthless. Anyone who disagreed with him was killed. In 1747 he was assassinated by religious leaders and army officers, who could stand his terrible cruelty no longer.

OTTOMAN EMPIRE

MIDDLE EAST

During the 1700s the rulers of the Ottoman Turks had to battle against enemies within and outside their empire. Sultan Ahmed III (ruled 1703–1730) spent the early years of his reign fighting the Russians. The war ended in 1711, when the Ottomans won. But Ahmed's next war, against Austria, ended in Turkish surrender. In 1730, after Persian ruler Nadir Shah had conquered a large area of Ottoman land, Ahmed was removed from power by the Janissaries, an elite regiment in his army. He died six years later.

Sultan Selim III (ruled 1789–1807) fought Russia, Great Britain, and powerful warlords in his own lands before he, too, was overthrown by the Janissaries. In 1807 they put him in prison, where he was murdered the next year.

CITY-STATES AND KINGDOMS

AFRICA

During the 1700s, West Africa was divided into many kingdoms and city-states, home to peoples such as the Hausa, the Yoruba, the Fulani, and the Bini. They were governed by powerful rulers, such as Usman dan Fodio (1754–1817), whose Fulani people conquered the Hausa lands in northern Nigeria. He and his followers were Muslims and set up an empire ruled by Muslim laws (see page 42).

A little farther south, the Bini people of Benin were led by rich kings called obas. Akenzua I, Eresoyen, and Akengbuda were also strong warriors, and eager to encourage trade in goods such as pepper, ivory, and fine brass work. Toward the end of Akengbuda's reign, his power faded, and Benin was weakened by civil wars.

INDIAN KINGDOMS

SOUTH ASIA

At this time large areas of India were controlled by British and French trading companies, but there were also many independent kingdoms, ruled by princes, peshwas (chief ministers), and religious leaders. These kingdoms sometimes fought among themselves and often clashed with the British. Hyder Ali became ruler of Mysore in southern India around 1760, after winning fame as a daring warrior. He conquered many nearby lands, but was defeated by the British in 1781 and died the next year. Hyder Ali's son, Tippu Sultan (ruled 1782–1799), continued his struggle.

◄ This gold head was made to decorate a royal stool used by Ashanti obas (kings) in West Africa. It is probably a portrait of an enemy ruler killed in battle.

▲ Gold monkey statues and curving roofs decorate Bangkok's Grand Palace. The palace was built for King Rama I.

BURMA AND SIAM

In 1752, Prince Alaungpaya of Burma (now Myanmar) defeated the Mons people, who had invaded northern Burma. In 1755 he established a new capital city at Rangoon (now Yangôn) and a year later won control of all Burma. He then became king, founding a new dynasty. In 1782, Chao Phraya Chakri became King of Siam (modern Thailand), taking the title Rama I. He made Bangkok the country's capital and built the Grand Palace and the Temple of the Emerald Buddha.

▼ Ambassadors from the Kirghiz people of far western China bringing valuable horses to present to Emperor Qianlong as tribute

EMPEROR QIANLONG

During the reign of Emperor Qianlong (ruled 1736–1796), China was rich and powerful, with a strong army, harsh laws, and a vast government bureaucracy. Qianlong's armies forced other East Asian states, including Korea, Burma, and Annam (present-day Vietnam) to pay tribute.

Like earlier Chinese rulers, Qianlong believed that China was a special "Middle Kingdom" at the center of the world, and that Chinese civilization was better than any other. In 1793 the British government sent Lord Macartney to China, to investigate possibilities for trade. But Qianlong refused to consider trade links. He said that China did not need to buy anything from elsewhere.

Qianlong ruled for 60 years, then retired. He did not think it right to reign for longer than his famous grandfather, Emperor Kangxi (ruled 1661–1722). But many people, both in China and outside, thought that Qianlong had been in power for too long. By the end of his reign, the government was short of money, its officials were inefficient, and the army was run down. The population was growing rapidly, and there were also food shortages in many parts of the empire.

GEORGE WASHINGTON

George Washington (1732–1799), the first President of the United States, was born into a wealthy, upper-class family. They lived in Virginia, then a British colony. Washington began his career as a soldier, fighting for the British against the French in the wars for control of American lands (see pages 16-17). By the age of 23, he had been promoted to the rank of colonel and appointed commander of Virginia's colonial troops. Next he went into politics By 1769 he was leading the growing opposition of American settlers to British colonial rule. Like many others of European ancestry, George Washington wanted independence for his country.

THE AMERICAN REVOLUTION

When the American Revolution broke out in 1775, Washington was chosen to lead the revolutionary army. He won great praise as a leader and for his quick thinking on the battlefield. After Britain was defeated, Washington retired for a while to his family estate at Mount Vernon, where he concentrated on farming, breeding horses and dogs, gardening, and business ventures. In 1787, with other famous politicians such as Benjamin Franklin, he took part in the discussions about the constitution for the newly independent nation. In 1789 he was unanimously elected president. By the time he died, ten years later, he was widely respected as "the Father of his Country."

▲ George Washington, the first President of the United States, shown with two symbols of his brilliant career. These are a sword, to show his success in battle, and a pen, to show that he helped to write the laws of the new country that he governed.

RESISTANCE AND REBELLION

In North America, Native American leaders such as Cornplanter (died 1836), chief of the Seneca, and Pontiac (c.1720–1769), chief of the Ottawas, fought against Europeans who had settled on their homelands. In South America, Tupac Amaru II, a descendant of the great Inca emperors who had once ruled Peru, led a rebellion against Spanish settlers from 1780 to 1781. On the Caribbean island of Haiti, a freed slave called Toussaint L'Ouverture (c.1743–1803) led a rebellion against the French in the 1790s. He and his followers demanded an end to slavery and freedom to run their country by themselves. They were supported by a group of French thinkers called *Les Amis des Noirs* (Friends of Black People). Toussaint was captured and taken to France, where he died in prison in 1803. But Haiti was granted independence the next year.

▼ Cornplanter, leader of the Native American Seneca people of the northeastern United States, painted in 1796. The artist has shown him wearing a feathered headdress and carrying a ceremonial tobacco pipe.

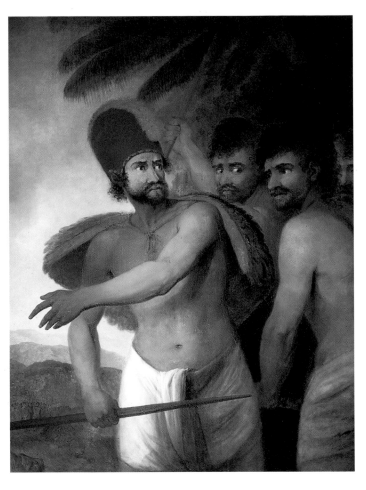

▲ A chief and two warriors from Hawaii, in the Pacific Ocean, as painted by a European artist who traveled there in 1787

HAWAIIAN ISLANDS

AUSTRALASIA

In the Pacific, King Kamehameha I (c.1758–1819) conquered most of the Hawaiian Islands and founded a new dynasty. The next four kings all had his name. King Kamehameha introduced new laws, fought against crime, and encouraged trade. He was interested to meet foreign sailors and explorers who visited Hawaii and was impressed by European technology. But he insisted on preserving Hawaii's ancient customs and traditional religious beliefs. He upheld the ancient system of taboos—laws that prohibited certain activities and relationships—and refused to let Christian missionaries land.

HOW PEOPLE LIVED

In some ways life in Marie Antoinette's time was much as it had been for hundreds of years. Food was still produced by farm laborers and most craft goods were still made by hand. There was still a great difference between the living standards of the wealthy few and of the ordinary masses, who were miserably poor. But there were also changes. The growth of international trade meant that foreign goods and ideas were spreading all around the world. European families wore Indian cotton. They drank hot chocolate made from American cocoa, sweetened with Caribbean sugar. Native Americans rode European horses and killed their prey with European knives. West African armies carried Portuguese muskets. By 1792, British sailors and traders were traveling as far as New Zealand to catch and sell whales.

▲ This elegant street was built in Vienna, the capital city of Austria, in the late 1700s. It is lined with many fashionable shops and cafes.

► This French political cartoon, produced at the time of the revolution (1789), shows a poor peasant weighed down by the taxes he pays to wealthy nobles and priests.

TOWN AND COUNTRY

EUROPE

In the 1700s most people lived in the country and earned their living from the land. Rich landowners lived in stately homes. Their wealth came from the woods, fields, and farms of their estates. Throughout the 1700s enterprising landowners experimented with stockbreeding and new farming methods, such as crop rotation, to make their land more productive. Peasants lived in tumbledown cottages and grew food for their families on their own plots of land, or worked as farm laborers on the estates of the rich.

But towns and cities were growing fast. Merchants, bankers, lawyers, doctors, and traders all lived there, as well as craft workers, who made goods such as cloth, cutlery, and shoes. In the biggest cities there were smart coffee shops, where men gathered to discuss business and politics and to read the newspapers. Many seaports also became wealthy as a result of increasing international trade.

► Many towns in the Middle East were important centers of trade. This colorful picture shows crowds shopping for all kinds of bargains in the souk (covered market) in Istanbul.

A HARD LIFE

MIDDLE EAST

In many parts of the Middle East, it was hard to make a living. Dry, scorching deserts in Arabia and high mountains and barren plains in parts of Turkey and Persia were all unsuited to growing crops. People survived by hunting desert animals, such as gazelles and rabbits, and by raising herds of camels or breeding hardy mountain sheep and goats. In the deserts the nomadic Bedouin people lived in tents woven from goat hair. In the mountains, villagers built well-defended houses from stone. In the marshlands of Iraq and the irrigated fields of Syria and Jordan, farmers grew a wide variety of crops. These included wheat, barley, beans, lettuce, melons, and chick peas. The inhabitants of these regions built their houses from sun-dried mud brick.

FARMERS, HERDERS, AND HUNTERS

AFRICA

African peoples at this time were mostly farmers, cattle herders, or hunters, depending on their environment. Farmers in the regions of present-day Zimbabwe and Tanzania grew millet and corn in the dry grasslands, while in Nigeria and Zaire, people planted crops of yams, okra, and plantains in the fields cleared from the hot, damp rain forest. They carried farm produce to market towns for sale to the local rulers, merchants, and craft workers who lived there.

Nomadic cattle herders spent their lives on the move, seeking water and grass for their animals. They lived mainly on milk, but sometimes drank fresh blood from live cattle. In the Kalahari Desert, the Khoikhoi people hunted wild animals and ate desert grubs. Close to the Cape of Good Hope, European settlers raised herds of cattle and planted corn and grapevines.

▼ This engraving shows the cattle-farming Dinka people, who lived (and still live) in southern present-day Sudan. In the background you can see the Dinkas' beehive-shaped homes.

SLAVERY

All around the coasts of Africa, people made a living by fishing or through trade. During the 1700s, the West African slave trade was at its height (see page 14). Under pressure from Europeans, African traders captured many people in raids. All were sold to European merchants as slaves and then shipped across the Atlantic Ocean to work in North and South America and the Caribbean islands. On the east coast, Arab traders also sold slaves to rich Arab and African families in Arabia, East Africa, and the island of Zanzibar.

INDIAN EXPORTS

SOUTH ASIA

By 1700, Indian farmers and craft workers had a long history of producing fine goods to sell. Indian spices had been carried overland to Europe since ancient Greek and Roman times. But during the 1700s many more Indians were involved in growing crops and making fabrics for export than ever before. Medicinal drugs like rhubarb and aloes (both used as laxatives) were in demand in Europe, as were spices like pepper and ginger. Indigo, a deep blue dye, was produced from plants grown on Indian farms. Indian workers grew, spun, wove, and printed many types of cotton, which fetched high prices in Europe. Much of this trade was controlled by European businessmen living in Indian towns. They worked for the British East India Company, or for similar groups based in France and the Netherlands.

CROPS AND CRAFTS

Indian farmers who did not produce goods for export grew food to feed their families and to sell at markets. Indian crops varied from region to region. In the north farmers kept cows and grew lentils and wheat. In the warmer, wetter south, they grew mangoes, coconuts, and rice. Other people made useful craft items, such as leather sandals, cooking pots, carpets, furniture, and bullock carts, to sell to ordinary people in India.

RICE GROWING

EAST ASIA

Rice was the staple food crop in most of East Asia. It was grown in flooded paddy fields, where young rice seedlings were planted in several inches of water. Villagers destroyed weeds by paddling barefoot in the water and stamping them into the mud. The ripe rice was harvested by hand, threshed, winnowed, polished, and stored in huge pottery jars that rats and mice could not gnaw through. In colder, northern regions (northern Korea and northern China), farmers grew wheat or barley instead of rice. Chili peppers were first imported from the Americas into parts of East Asia around 1700 and soon became a popular crop.

▲ This wide cotton belt, decorated with stencilled and hand-painted flowers, was made in northwestern India around 1700.

CITY LIFE

In the 1700s most Japanese houses were made of wood. As there were frequent earthquakes in the country, the interior walls were movable, lightweight screens made of paper and bamboo. This meant that they would not crush people inside if the houses fell down.

Japanese cities were packed with these wooden houses. Smoking was officially banned because of the risk of fire. But in fact the habit was very popular, especially in the pleasure districts known as floating worlds that were attached to big cities. There citizens ate, drank, went to concerts and the theater (see page 38), and watched sumo wrestling. They also relaxed in public bath-houses, played cards and board games, and enjoyed the company of beautiful, well-educated women, who were known as geishas.

◀ A Japanese audience enjoying a play in a kabuki theater in 1745. The theater has several stage platforms and is lit by paper lanterns.

▲ This stately home, called Monticello, was designed in the European style by the third President of the United States, Thomas Jefferson. Only the richest Americans could afford homes like this. Many ordinary farmers lived in log cabins.

EUROPEAN SETTLERS

AMERICAS

European settlers in North and South America had two main goals. These were to build new communities, run according to European political (and sometimes religious) ideas, and to make their fortunes. They cut down forests and cleared fields to create farms. They grew corn and other vegetables, planted orchards, and raised chickens, pigs, and cows. In the colonies of the American South, wealthier settlers had huge plantations, where they grew tobacco, rice, and cotton. Black slaves transported from West Africa, then sold to plantation owners at auctions, carried out all the heavy work in the fields. There were also enormous, European-owned estates in the Caribbean islands, where gangs of slaves harvested sugar cane and made it into sugar. It was then shipped to Europe to be sold.

NATIVE PEOPLES

Elsewhere Native Americans continued to live as they had done for thousands of years. In the high Andes Mountains of South America, peasant farmers grew potatoes and raised herds of llamas and alpacas. On the Pacific coast of Canada, fishing communities caught salmon and harpooned seals and whales. But slowly these lifestyles were changed through contact with Europeans. In both North and South America, Native Americans were driven from their lands when European settlers arrived and took over their fields, woods, and hunting grounds. They had to adapt quickly to new, less hospitable environments, where their old hunting, farming, or fishing skills were of little use. Sometimes they had to fight Native peoples already living in their "new" territory, to win a share of their land.

▼ South American people harvesting corn on a settler's estate. In many parts of South America, Europeans owned the best farming land, so Native Americans had to work for them.

ISLAND LIFE

AUSTRALASIA

Australasia was a land of islands. The enormous continent of Australia itself was inhabited by Aborigines, who followed an ancient lifestyle based on hunting and gathering wild food. There were also over 3,000 smaller islands scattered across the Pacific Ocean. The peoples who lived there came from many different places and spoke hundreds of different languages. But their lives were similar. They grew sweet potatoes, yams, bananas, pumpkins, breadfruit, and an edible root called taro; kept pigs; and caught fish and shellfish in coral lagoons. Most were expert sailors and traveled across the ocean using the sun, stars, and clouds to navigate. They were also skilled boatbuilders and woodworkers, who made log canoes decorated with elaborate carvings.

▲ This peaceful view of the island of Tahiti, in the South Pacific Ocean, was painted by a European artist in 1792. It shows Tahitian people climbing trees to gather coconuts and going fishing in canoes.

NEW ZEALAND

The Maori people of New Zealand lived in wooden-walled villages surrounded by vegetable gardens, where they grew kumara (an orange-fleshed sweet potato). The Maori also gathered wild bracken roots, which they dried, ground, and boiled with water to make a food. They hunted bats, rats, kiwis, and moas—huge, flightless birds—and they made vast nets to catch eels and fish on the seashore. They also gathered seaweed and shellfish to eat and hunted for whales. Like other Pacific islanders, the Maori sometimes also ate the bodies of enemies captured in battle.

DISCOVERY AND INVENTION

Many people in Marie Antoinette's time devoted their lives to seeking new knowledge. Some, like British explorer Captain James Cook, traveled right around the world on their quest. Others, like American inventor Benjamin Franklin, performed dangerous experiments to investigate natural forces such as heat and electricity. Some scientists climbed mountains or combined alarming mixtures of chemicals to try to discover how rocks, metals, and even the air we breathe were made. Others found new, more accurate ways of measuring things—from the size and shape of the universe to the passing of time.

▲ John Harrison's chronometer was a breakthrough in scientific timekeeping. No watch or clock had ever been as accurate before. Harrison designed several versions of his chronometer. This one was made in 1759.

NEW IDEAS

EUROPE

The scientific ideas of the Enlightenment (see page 41) led to a huge number of new inventions and discoveries in many parts of Europe. It was fashionable—and could be profitable—to be a scientist, doctor, or engineer. Noblemen collected science books for their libraries. Learned societies were founded, where leading scholars gave lectures. Inventors and mechanics conducted experiments to make new materials and machines.

Inventions, like the coke process for smelting iron (1709), James Hargreaves's spinning jenny for mass-producing woolen thread (patented, 1770), and James Watt's steam engine (1765), helped new industries develop fast. Some discoveries were breakthroughs in understanding. About 1780, Frenchman Antoine Lavoisier discovered that air is made up mostly of the gases oxygen and nitrogen, while in 1790, Italian Luigi Galvani made progress toward discovering how electricity works.

▲ In France during the 1700s, the Montgolfier brothers designed hot-air balloons powerful enough to lift people off the ground. The first flew near Paris in 1783.

TIME AND TEMPERATURE

Scientists in the 1700s also devised better ways of measuring time and temperature. For example, in 1714, German physicist Gabriel Fahrenheit invented the first accurate thermometer. In 1762, British clockmaker John Harrison perfected his chronometer. It enabled sailors in vast oceans, out of sight of land, to calculate their precise position.

In 1735 a new system for classifying plants and animals into different species was also developed. Swedish botanist Carolus Linnaeus showed how many seemingly different creatures (for example, cats and lions) are related, because of the way their bodies are made. His system is still used today.

◄ The spinning jenny was a machine that could spin fine, strong, even thread much faster and more cheaply than it was possible to do by hand. Machines such as this paved the way for the Industrial Revolution about the mid 1700s.

DEADLY DISEASE

Smallpox was a highly infectious disease that spread through many countries in Marie Antoinette's time. Over half the people who caught it died. In 1719, English traveler Lady Mary Wortley Montagu reported on a treatment to prevent the disease that she had seen in Istanbul. Turkish doctors took infected matter from a smallpox patient and rubbed it into scratches on healthy people's arms. Then they tied a walnut shell over the scratches and waited for the disease to take hold. Most patients developed a mild form of smallpox, which protected them from getting the disease in the future. But at least two in every 100 caught a severe form and died. After reading Lady Mary's report, European doctors copied this method of inoculation, testing it on orphans and prisoners. Then, in 1721, British king George I allowed two of his grandchildren to be inoculated. At the end of the century, British doctor Edward Jenner made inoculation safer by using matter from patients with cowpox, a similar but less dangerous disease.

ADVENTUROUS JOURNEYS

Before 1750 few Europeans dared to travel inland in Africa. Toward the end of the century, however, two pioneering expeditions did set off. Both were led by Scotsmen inspired by scientific curiosity to explore Africa's great rivers. In 1768, James Bruce began a five-year journey through Egypt and Ethiopia to search for the source of the Nile River. In 1795, Mungo Park set off to explore the Gambia and the Niger River.

▶ This dramatic engraving was made in 1860 to illustrate a copy of Mungo Park's book about his expedition of 1795. He returned to West Africa to continue exploring in 1805, but was drowned the next year.

◀ Lady Mary Wortley Montagu spent many years in the Middle East. Here she is shown wearing Turkish-style dress.

JAI SINGH

In India, Rajput ruler Jai Singh (died 1743) was a skillful politician and brave soldier. But he was even more respected for his scientific skills as a mathematician, astronomer, architect, and town planner. Jai Singh built five huge observatories to study the stars and sent a team of experts to meet and discuss astronomy with European scholars. He studied traditional Indian mathematics, as well as Greek and Arabic scientific writings. And he built a new capital city, Jaipur, planning its layout himself after studying many other cities in India and abroad.

▲ This massive observatory was built near Delhi, India, by the scholarly prince Jai Singh.

MEDICAL MARVELS

EAST ASIA

During Marie Antoinette's time Chinese emperor Qianlong (see page 21) gave orders for all traditional Chinese medical knowledge to be collected in a huge, multi-volume encyclopedia. This was called *The Golden Mirror of Medicine* and was completed about 1743.

For many centuries Japanese doctors had studied Chinese medicine and used it to treat their patients. But during the lifetime of medical reformer Goto Konzan (1659–1733), many new treatments began to be introduced. Goto believed that all disease was caused by stagnant "life force" in the body. His new therapies were designed to get this life force flowing freely again.

▶ This Chinese medical diagram, which was drawn during the 1700s, shows how to use a traditional Chinese method of healing called acupuncture to treat people suffering from heart disease.

THE BERING STRAIT

EAST ASIA

In 1728 and 1733 the Russian government gave Danish explorer Vitus Bering (1681–1741) permission to explore the Siberian coast. He mapped large areas of the coastline and explored the channel that runs between Siberia and Alaska. Today it is still called the Bering Strait. A Russian explorer, Semyon Dezhnyov, had reached Alaska in 1648, but his journey had been forgotten. Until Bering's voyages, no European scientists or governments knew that Alaska existed.

HORSE POWER

AMERICAS

Horses were introduced to the Americas from Europe in the 1500s. During the 1700s they caused a transportation revolution among Native Americans living on the Great Plains. Horses allowed them to travel greater distances than ever before. Hunters no longer had to stay within a few days' walking distance of their homes, but could follow buffalo herds many hundreds of miles across the plains. Before this time many Plains people had lived in villages for several months each year. Horses made it possible for some to develop a nomadic lifestyle, traveling most of the time and living in camps of easily transportable, buffalo-hide tepees.

SCIENTIFIC IDEAS

Americans whose ancestors came from Europe were interested in new European political and scientific ideas. In the 1700s they founded many libraries, colleges, and schools. European scientific books were sent to America, but American scientists also made their own discoveries. Benjamin Franklin (1706–1790) carried out experiments with electricity and invented the lightning rod, a stove, and bifocal lenses.

Other American scientists invented machines designed to help farmers. In 1793, Eli Whitney invented a cotton gin (*gin* is short for *engine*) that removed the fibers from the seed heads of the cotton plant. This made it cheaper and easier to produce cotton thread. American engineers like John Fitch and Robert Fulton experimented with designs for new, steam-powered boats.

▼ In a dangerous experiment that involved flying a kite into a thunderstorm, American statesman Benjamin Franklin proved that lightning is a form of electricity.

◀ In New Zealand, Maori farmers built storehouses raised high above the ground on wooden legs to keep rats and flightless birds from stealing their crops. They decorated their homes and storehouses with beautiful carvings. This storehouse is covered with patterns showing humans fighting against bird-spirits, which were Maori symbols of life and death.

THREE EXPLORERS

From 1721 to 1722, Dutchman Jacob Roggeveen explored Samoa and the Solomon Islands. He was probably also the first European to explore mysterious Easter Island. Although the island was deserted, the colossal statues on its shores showed that it had once been home to a wealthy community. From 1766 to 1769, French scientist Louis Bougainville sailed right around the world, visiting many Pacific islands. He investigated the structure of the earth—its rocks, mountains, and volcanoes—as well as the plants and animals he saw. Between 1768 and 1779, British explorer Captain James Cook made three voyages to the region, visiting Eastern Australia, New Zealand, New Caledonia, Tonga, and the Hawaiian Islands. He took specially trained artists with him to record everything of scientific interest that he observed.

PACIFIC PEOPLES

AUSTRALASIA

As the peoples of Australia, New Zealand, and the Pacific kept no written records, it is difficult to find out whether they made any new inventions or discoveries during the 1700s. But European travelers who met them reported that they had many ingenious ways of farming, hunting, and fishing and that they built fine houses and canoes. Europeans also described the traditional customs of the Pacific peoples. Some of these, such as cannibalism, horrified them. Others, like bravery and hospitality, they very much admired.

▶ This scorpion fish from the Pacific Ocean was painted by Sydney Parkinson, one of the artists who accompanied Captain Cook on his first scientific voyage around the world, from 1768 to 1771. As well as paintings like this, Cook brought home shells, bones, fossils, and many plant specimens.

THE CREATIVE WORLD

In Marie Antoinette's time the arts—painting, sculpture, architecture, music, dance, and theater—were designed to impress. Palaces, paintings, statues, plays, concerts, and operas were all meant to show their creators' skill and the wealth and good taste of the kings, queens, and other powerful people who paid vast sums for them. Far from the stately homes and big cities, among ordinary people, the arts had many other purposes. They formed part of important ceremonies and events, such as marriages, funerals, farming festivals, and even preparations for warfare. Growing naturally out of everyday life, they bound people and communities together.

▲ A gala concert celebrating a royal wedding in the palace of Empress Maria Theresa. The audience are listening to the young musician and composer Wolfgang Amadeus Mozart, aged 5, playing the harpsichord.

◀ This bronze disc commemorates the founding of St. Petersburg by Czar (Emperor) Peter the Great in 1703.

PRECIOUS TREASURES

Powerful Middle Eastern rulers paid for top artists and craftspeople to produce wonderful works of art for their palaces. The Ottoman emperors of Turkey collected silk carpets, painted ceramics, gold and silver dishes, and glittering swords encrusted with rubies and diamonds. When Persian ruler Nadir Shah invaded India in 1739, he seized the world's most famous diamond—the massive Koh-i-noor (mountain of light)—to add to his royal treasury.

COLORFUL COSTUMES

Ordinary people in the Middle East embroidered their clothes using wool or cotton colored with vegetable dyes. Some women wore headdresses and necklaces of silver coins. In country areas with no banks, this was the best way to look after their savings. Nomadic peoples also decorated their tents, carpets, and even the saddlebags of horses and camels with elaborate geometric designs.

▼ An Ottoman royal hunting party in the 1700s. The sultan, in the center, is seated on a rich carpet and embroidered cushions.

ART FOR RICH AND POOR

During the 1700s some of Europe's grandest palaces, including Schönbrunn in Austria and Buckingham Palace in England, were built. Elegant new towns, such as Williamsburg in the United States, Bath in England, and St. Petersburg in Russia, were also constructed. Artists like Frenchwoman Élisabeth Vigée-Lebrun and Englishman Sir Joshua Reynolds painted stylish portraits, while Frenchman Antoine Watteau and Englishman Thomas Gainsborough painted beautiful landscapes. In Austria and Hungary, composers Wolfgang Amadeus Mozart and Franz Joseph Haydn wrote brilliant music. German composer George Frideric Handel moved to England, where he wrote operas and also *Messiah*, a famous choral work.

The arts admired by the wealthy few were not available to ordinary people. They could not enter the picture galleries and music rooms of grand houses. They could not afford books or tickets to operas and plays. Instead they enjoyed folk songs, country dances, ballads, and rude cartoons that mocked the rich and powerful.

BRASS FROM BENIN

AFRICA

In West Africa highly skilled brassworkers from the kingdom of Benin made portrait heads of important people and brass plaques that recorded traditional stories and important events. These were used to decorate the palace of the oba (king) in the center of the city of Benin. In the nearby Ashanti kingdom, metalworkers made hundreds of tiny brass weights. These were used for weighing gold dust, the Ashanti people's chief wealth. In central and southern Africa, some of the best craft workers and artists made religious carvings and masks, or clothes and jewelry.

◀ The Ashanti made brass weights in the shape of everyday objects, like this man on a horse. Sometimes the weights were decorated with magical or holy patterns, too.

INDIAN MINIATURES

SOUTH ASIA

By 1700 there was already a long tradition of painting miniatures in India. These were tiny, very precise paintings in glowing colors and full of fascinating details. Often they were decorated with an ornate border. Many were designed to be pasted into albums, where they could be kept safe and admired. Elsewhere in South Asia, craft workers produced fine textiles and metalwork. On the Indonesian islands of Java and Bali, most men carried a type of dagger called a kris. If they could afford it, they had the handle decorated with elaborate designs.

KABUKI CULTURE

EAST ASIA

In Japan, kabuki theater was one of the most popular art forms. It had been invented about 1603 by a woman entertainer called Okuni, but by the 1700s was performed only by men. Kabuki plays were exciting, with lots of action, elaborate costumes, and special effects using revolving stages and trapdoors. Kabuki actors sang and danced, in addition to speaking. They were accompanied by an on-stage orchestra. (See page 27.) Many traditional stories were used as plots for plays. But in the 1700s, dramatist Tsuruya Namboku IV created the first kabuki "gangster" plays, about thieves and murderers. Audiences loved them!

▼ This Indian miniature, painted around 1770, shows a princess in a beautiful garden, surrounded by peacocks. She is carrying a lute.

◄ This painting, in "primitive" American settler style, shows people and animals living together in an imaginary world. Pictures like this reflected the settlers' wish to build a godly and peaceful kingdom in their new homeland.

TRADITION AND CHANGE

AMERICAS

By the 1700s, Native Americans living in both North and South America had been making art objects for hundreds of years. They ranged from massive stone temples to fragile pottery and delicate jewels. Each group had its own artistic styles. Many of these traditions continued throughout the 1700s, but others changed under the influence of new materials, techniques, and designs brought by Europeans who had settled in American lands.

OLD STONE, NEW BEADS

In South America and the southern United States, Christian missionaries built churches and monasteries. Sometimes they used the stones of earlier non-Christian temples for their buildings. In North America, European traders sold brightly colored glass beads to Native American women living in the Northeast and on the Great Plains. The women used these beads to decorate clothes, belts, shoes, and headdresses. They were longer-lasting, easier to sew, and much quicker to obtain than the porcupine quills that had traditionally been used for these items.

SETTLER STYLES

European settler artists and craft workers developed their own new styles and techniques. American folk artists created paintings in a deliberately plain style that was influenced by their simple lifestyle and forms of religious worship. In remote country districts there were no shops, so settler women often had to recycle material. They created beautiful patchwork quilts from old scraps of cloth.

PACIFIC ARTS

AUSTRALASIA

When the first European explorers reached the Pacific islands, they were fascinated by the arts and crafts of the local peoples. European travelers recorded seeing tattoos and body paintings in graceful, swirling designs, sculptures of gods and goddesses made from shells, sharks' teeth, wood, and stone, and carved doorways on the houses of chiefs.

In Australia, Aborigine artists continued their ancient traditions of cave painting and rock engraving. Another important art form was the telling of traditional stories, often through dance and song. In this way elders passed on the history of their people, as well as their ideas and beliefs.

BELIEFS AND IDEAS

Are old ideas always right? Should people always value ancient beliefs or be prepared to replace them? Do scientific laws or mysterious forces control the world? Are calm discussions or dramatic revolutions the best way to bring about change? All these questions—and many more—faced people during the 1700s. Suddenly new scientific discoveries and political ideas were challenging the views held by rulers, scholars, and religious leaders for centuries. In many different parts of the world, important people responded to these challenges in many different ways. Some strengthened their traditional beliefs and ideas. Others hurried to accept the new.

▲ In 1766, British artist and scientist Joseph Wright of Derby painted this dramatic picture of an astronomer and his family with an orrery—a model of the earth, sun, moon, and planets.

CHRISTIAN BELIEFS

EUROPE

In Europe during the 1700s, most people called themselves Christians. But there were many varieties of the Christian faith. Marie Antoinette, her family in Austria, and most of the people she ruled in France were Roman Catholics. Most Spanish and Italian people were Catholics, too. But in England, Germany, and Scandinavia, the majority of people were Protestants. They disagreed with some Roman Catholic beliefs and ways of worship.

JOHN WESLEY

By 1700 new religious movements were calling for church reforms. John Wesley (1703–1791) was a priest in the Church of England and a university teacher. He became leader of a group of Christians nicknamed "Methodists." Wesley encouraged people to worship in a direct, simple way. He traveled around Britain and to the U.S. preaching in the open air, founded Methodist chapels, wrote books on religion, and composed rousing hymns. His preaching alarmed Church of England authorities, but attracted many followers.

◄ The sermons of preacher John Wesley appealed to ordinary people who did not normally go to church.

► A decorated copy of the Qur'an. Muslim reformers in the 1700s wanted people to concentrate on the meaning of the Qur'an's holy words rather than on admiring beautiful pages like these.

THE ENLIGHTENMENT

At the same time the Methodists were winning support, traditional Christianity in Europe was being challenged by a new movement based on scientific, deliberately nonreligious ideas. Members of this movement, known as the Enlightenment, sought the truth by relying on human intelligence, rather than religious beliefs. The movement was strongest in France and Germany, but there were supporters elsewhere. Members believed that their search for truth would improve people's lives. French thinker Jean Jacques Rousseau planned new forms of education designed to teach people to live simply and honestly. In 1780, Frenchman Denis Diderot completed a 35-volume encyclopedia, containing all the latest discoveries and ideas.

ISLAMIC IDEAS

MIDDLE EAST

During the 1700s most people in the Middle East were Muslims. Muhammad ibn Abd al–Wahhab (1703–1792) wanted them to return to older, purer ways of worship. In his Book of Unity, he called for worship to be based only on the Qur'an, the Muslim holy book, and for governments to base their laws on *sharia,* the Muslim holy law.

BAAL SHEM TOV

Jewish leader Baal Shem Tov (c.1700–1760) distrusted the form of Judaism taught by the top scholars of his day. He called for Jewish people to return to the basis of their religion—total devotion to God. He taught them to worship God simply, through eager prayers and joyful singing and dancing, and to oppose the scholars' reforms. Baal Shem Tov's ideas became popular among poor people in country areas of Eastern Europe and the Middle East. Later they developed into a branch of Judaism called Hasidism, which still exists today.

HOLY WAR

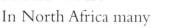

In North Africa many people were Muslims. There were also centers of Islamic learning in the region, such as the cities of Djenné and Timbuktu. But many African Muslims lived in countries where the laws and customs were based on traditional, non-Muslim beliefs. During the 1700s leaders such as Usman dan Fodio (1754–1817) called for the purification of African Islam. He led a jihad (holy war) against the rulers of present-day northern Nigeria. Once they were defeated, he set up a kingdom modeled on the first Muslim empire and governed by religious laws based on the Qur'an.

TRADITIONAL BELIEFS

In the rest of Africa, people continued to follow traditional beliefs. These included honoring their dead ancestors and making offerings of food and objects to the magical spirits, gods, and goddesses who were believed to watch over different aspects of life. For example, in the West African kingdom of Benin, women made offerings at little shrines dedicated to Olokun, the god of fertility, wealth, and good fortune. To protect their families, they made shrines to the god Esu outside their homes. They believed Esu would drive away evil.

▲ A Jewish marriage contract from the 1700s. Baal Shem Tov wanted religion to play a part in every stage of life.

HINDU WORSHIP

Although large areas of India were ruled by Muslim Mogul emperors, the majority of the population were Hindus. There were also communities of Buddhists, Muslims, Sikhs, Jains, and Parsees. Hinduism is a very ancient faith. Over the centuries many styles of Hindu worship developed. In the 1700s a way of worshiping called bhakti was popular. It encouraged ordinary Hindus to take a direct part in religious ceremonies, rather than leaving prayers and rituals to scholars, holy men, and priests. Ordinary people joined in prayers, processions, and pilgrimages. They sang religious songs using everyday language rather than ancient Sanskrit, which few understood.

As British power in India grew, British people began to criticize Hinduism. This led to mistrust between Britons and Indians of many faiths.

▲ The Golden Temple at Amritsar, India, is the Sikhs' most important religious center. The temple holds the *Granth Sahib*, the Sikhs' holy book. When Guru Gobind Singh died, he said that there would be no more gurus. Instead he told people to read the *Granth Sahib* for guidance.

▼ Villagers worshiping Hindu gods at a holy place in the Himalaya Mountains. This picture was painted by a European about 1800.

SIKH WARRIORS

The Sikh religion was founded in the Punjab region of northern India around 1500. During the 1700s, Sikh warriors fought to protect their faith. They were led by Guru Gobind Singh (died 1708) and Prince Ranjit Singh (1780–1839). Guru Gobind Singh, the last of the Sikhs' Great Gurus (religious leaders), battled against persecution by Mogul emperors. Ranjit Singh struggled to achieve independence for Sikh lands.

CLOSED COUNTRIES

EAST ASIA

Throughout the 1700s, China and Japan were both almost entirely cut off from contact with the other nations of the world (see page 16). This was their rulers' own decision. They thought of all outsiders, and particularly Europeans, as "foreign devils," and they did not want them to spread alien ideas and religions, such as Christianity, among their people.

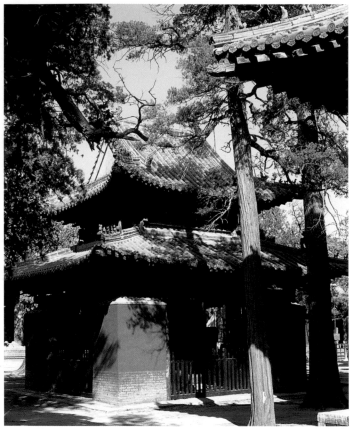

▲ This temple in the city of Qufu, China, was built to honor the ancient philosopher Confucius.

RELIGIOUS BELIEFS

EAST ASIA

For Chinese and Japanese rulers, and for many ordinary Chinese and Japanese people as well, their religion was linked to their sense of national pride. Most Chinese people followed the teachings of Confucius, a philosopher who lived around 500 B.C. He taught people to honor their parents and teachers and to treat one another with respect. On the emperor's orders, the temple at Confucius's birthplace at Qufu in the state of Lu was rebuilt in 1724.

In Japan, Shinto was the most widespread religion. It was based on the worship of sacred spirits. They were believed to be all around—in the souls of great leaders, in gods and goddesses, in holy places such as Mount Fuji, and even in rocks, lakes, rivers, and streams.

SHARED IDEAS

AMERICAS

Each Native American group had its own holy myths and legends, religious faith, and ways of worship. But almost all their religions had ideas in common. They shared a belief in Mother Earth and a reverence for all living things. They believed that sacrifices, and sometimes suffering, might persuade the gods and spirits to help them. They also believed that priests and healers called shamans had the power to communicate with the spirits, through prayers, meditation, music, and dancing. People hoped that the shamans' skills would bring them good fortune in their lives, or at least drive away bad luck.

◄ Native Americans from northeastern North America made masks from carved wood and animal hair to wear at special religious ceremonies. These were thought to protect people and their homes from harm, and to cure sickness.

THE DELAWARE PROPHET

During the 1700s several Native American shamans felt inspired to lead their people against the European settlers. For example, the Delaware Prophet (his real name is unknown) began to preach in northeastern North America about 1762. He said that he had received a vision of a glorious new future. If Native Americans returned to their traditional ways of life and gave up their guns and everything else they had purchased or copied from Europeans, they would grow strong again. This would enable them to drive the foreigners from their lands. A few powerful Native American leaders, for example Pontiac (see page 23), followed some of the Delaware Prophet's advice. But, tragically, the glorious new future he had promised never arrived.

▲ Pacific islanders, like these men from Hawaii, made offerings to gods and spirits. This was a way of asking for their help and protection.

SUPERNATURAL POWER

In many parts of the Pacific, kings and chiefs relied on supernatural power, which they called mana, to help them rule. They and their subjects believed that mana was given by the gods to certain chosen people, as a reward for goodness, bravery, or wisdom. A ruler who had mana won extra respect, because it would help him to achieve success in wars or to govern his people well. Mana could also belong to objects, such as statues of the gods, or to holy places, where powerful spirits were worshiped.

GLOSSARY

PEOPLES FROM AROUND THE WORLD

Aborigines The first inhabitants of Australia, who arrived there about 40,000 years ago.

Ashanti Farmers, traders, and skilled metalworkers who lived in the region of present-day Ghana.

Bambara Warriors and cattle herders who lived in the region of present-day Mali.

Bini (also called Edo) Farmers and traders who lived in the kingdom of Benin, in the region of present-day Nigeria.

Buganda (also called Ganda) Farmers and hunters who lived in the region of present-day Uganda.

Dinka Nomadic cattle herders who lived in the region of present-day southern Sudan and in the Rift Valley area to the south.

Fulani Cattle herders and town builders who lived in the region of present-day Chad, Senegal, and western Sudan.

Hausa Farmers, craft workers, and traders who lived in the region of present-day northern and central Nigeria.

Khoikhoi Nomadic hunters and gatherers who lived in southwestern Africa.

Kirghiz Semi-nomadic farmers who raised sheep and goats in wild regions of Central Asia.

Luanda (also called Mbundu) Farmers and hunters who lived in the region of present-day Angola and nearby lands.

Maori Settlers in New Zealand who arrived there from the Pacific islands about A.D. 800.

Marathas A powerful people, led by warrior princes, who lived in central India.

Masai Cattle herders and hunters who lived in and around the region of present-day Kenya.

Mons Rice farmers who lived in the region of present-day Thailand and Myanmar.

Native Americans The first inhabitants of America, who arrived there about 30,000 years ago. Native American people were divided into many groups.

Ottawa Native American traders, hunters, and farmers who lived in northern North America.

Seneca Native American peoples who lived as hunters and farmers in present-day New York State and eastern Ohio.

Xhosa Cattle farmers who lived in the region of present-day Transkei, South Africa.

Yoruba Farmers and traders who lived in the region of present-day Nigeria and Benin.

acupuncture A system of Chinese medicine intended to cure illness by placing needles under the skin to balance forces within the body.

alliance A friendly agreement between nations.

auction A sale in which buyers make bids (offers of money) for goods. The highest bid wins.

ballad A song that tells a story.

bamboo A plant that looks rather like giant grass. Its stems and leaves are used for building.

bifocal lenses Specially shaped pieces of glass used in spectacles. They allow wearers to see both close and distant objects.

breadfruit A large, round, heavy tropical fruit with starchy flesh.

bureaucracy A system of government that relies on large numbers of well-trained officials to collect taxes and enforce laws.

cannibalism The eating of people by other people, often as part of religious ceremonies.

cavalry Soldiers on horseback.

ceramics Beautiful objects—pots, tiles, and statues—made of clay.

chapel A small Christian church.

choral work A piece of music performed by many people singing together in a choir.

city-state A city that also rules the surrounding countryside.

civil war Fighting between groups in the same country.

colonize To establish settlers in a distant land and govern them from the homeland.

colony A country that has been colonized (see page 46).

confederation An alliance (see page 46) between a group of friendly, equal nations or peoples.

constitution A set of rules and laws for governing a country.

crop rotation Changing the crops grown in fields each year, to stop the buildup of pests and allow the soil to regain its fertility.

dynasty A ruling family.

empire A large area of land, including several different nations or peoples, that is governed by a single ruler called an emperor.

engraving A picture produced by printing from an image cut into a wooden block or metal plate.

estate A large area of land owned by a single family.

fossil The remains of a living creature millions of years old that have been hardened.

Holy Roman Emperor An ancient title belonging to a European royal family. It was abolished in 1806.

Industrial Revolution The time (from around 1750 to 1900) of change in northern Europe and North America in which steam power and new machines were invented, new factories and towns were built, and new forms of transportation developed.

inoculation A way of protecting people against serious disease by deliberately infecting them with a milder form of the same illness.

irrigation Channeling water to dry land so crops can grow there.

kimono A long, loose robe with wide sleeves worn in Japan.

lightning rod A metal rod fixed on tall buildings to carry the electricity from lightning safely down to the ground.

meditation Thinking deeply about spiritual things.

millet A food crop that is related to rice and other grains.

missionary A person who travels to another country to spread his or her religious beliefs.

monastery A religious community where monks live apart from the world.

Mother Earth The earth viewed as a goddess who feeds and provides for her people.

musket A type of firearm.

navigation The skill and science of steering a course at sea.

nomadic Moving from place to place in search of food or of grazing land for animals.

okra A vegetable that has small, edible pods with soft flesh.

philosopher A person who studies knowledge and wisdom.

pilgrimage A special journey to visit a holy place.

plantain A green, bananalike fruit cooked as a vegetable.

plantation Land where crops, such as cotton or sugar cane, are grown.

plaque A piece of carved metal or stone, usually fixed to a wall.

reform A change intended to improve something.

regent A person who rules on behalf of a king or queen.

regiment A group of soldiers.

republic A country ruled by elected leaders, not a monarch.

savannah Grassland.

smelt To crush then heat rocks containing metal until the metal melts and runs out.

stockbreeding A way of improving farm animals, such as cows, by breeding only the fittest.

sumo wrestling A popular Japanese sport perfomed by very large, strong wrestlers.

sweet potato A yellow-fleshed root cooked as a vegetable.

taboo Things set apart as forbidden. The idea of "taboo" forms part of the religious beliefs of many Pacific islanders.

taro A fleshy root cooked as a vegetable.

tepee An animal-skin tent made by some Native Americans.

thresh To separate grains and seeds from plant stalks, usually by hitting them with a large stick.

treason The crime of betraying one's country or ruler.

tribute Forced payment by one ruler to another.

warlord A warrior leader who controls parts of a country.

winnow To separate grains and seeds from their casing, often by throwing them up into the air.

yam A root that is cooked and eaten as a vegetable.

INDEX